Passage of Souls
Poems of Philosophical Design

Victoria Porcello Meghdir

**Dedicated with Love
to Hamou**

**with appreciation
for his encouragement and support**

TABLE OF CONTENTS

Chapter 1

Poems of Philosophical Idealism

Heaven or Hell

For future reward or fear of punishment should one be kind?
No, recompense is earthly, whether with malice or peace of mind.

Better to shun anger, for one does reap what is sown,
Heaven or hell is invoked by our actions alone.

Damnation's sorry is caused here among the living,
The torments of the harmful and mean remain unforgiving.

The solution is at hand though, worthy to promote,
To embrace the Golden Rule, so simple yet so remote.

Eudaimonia
(Happiness through Virtue and Moderation)

How very clever they could be
Some ancient Greeks from times B.C.

Nearly 3,000 years ago their influence extended wide
To hundreds of Mediterranean colonies, trade and arts they supplied

Advanced ideas in medicine, math and astronomy flourished
The higher pursuits of mind and body were nourished

These three especially stand out: Socrates, Plato, Aristotle for sure
Philosophy, the greatest undertaking, the most sublime and pure

Summum bonum, the highest good, the loftiest human activity
An ethical journey toward "Eudaimonia" was their proclivity

"The good indwelling spirit" from personal growth, benefiting others,
Health, wealth, beauty and treating men as brothers

The purpose of Philosophy is to find meaning in one's life
Ignorance and lack of virtue cause all evils and strife

The ideal goal: happiness through virtue and moderation,
Being one's best self, the immortal soul's inspiration

Man is gifted with capacities beyond those shared with vegetation
Wisdom and knowledge cultivate one's character and motivation

Acting in a virtuous manner makes goodness a habit,
Inspires others and attracts more goodness, from this we all profit.

Supernal Quest

If only I could find
The perfect words to define
A certain feeling almost divine

It walks without touching the ground
It talks with and without sound
It radiates warmth all around

Hopeful for mankind
Uplifting the weary mind
Understanding and always kind

Rising far above petty irritation
Striving for positive innovation
Assuring calm appreciation

Causing tears to unexpectedly stream
At a beautiful or tender scene
Or helping the defenseless against all that is mean

An emotion of elation
The armor needed for protection
Against a world of imperfection

The Table where Beauty is Served

The elation of those memorable moments flows fleetingly by,
the undesirable lingers on, relived over and again.
Our nature's normal response is to focus on the affliction,
The disagreeable often overshadows the taken-for-granted gain.

A claret mark spilled on a cream-colored cloth
screams out its presence, impossible to ignore,
marring the surrounding spectacle, usurping the attention
meant for the table's gleaming finery.

Resist the lure of this pervasive pirate
this pilferer of pleasure and peace of mind.
Bend its grip on our sensitive senses.
Cover the flaw with lace!
Eradicate it with loveliness.

Minify the imperfections
lest they color all the rest.
Instead of the failing,
see only the bountiful feast.

The Spirit of Motivation

Poke constantly at that fire
Stoke it with more wood
Fix your attention on keeping it lit
Fixating on its destructive path
Give in to its consuming allure
until it burns your brow
singeing your hair
permeating your skin with a sooty scent
choking away your oxygen

This is what people do to their brain
when they wallow, bemoan and complain
focusing on dreary thoughts
reinforcing a habit of discontent
skewed perception cemented by conviction
ungrateful and uninformed

Break away instead
from the sad smoldering embers
to focus on all that you do have
not what is missing
breathe fresh air, get up and get out
alter those thoughts by physical effort
walking, running, dancing away
decide to like your life
energize your existence

Continued

If you still feel blasé and uninspired
you are not considering
the millions of years of evolution and effort
that have brought us to such a privileged point
Are you cold, hungry, parasite infested, disease ridden?
Do you have to battle beasts?
Or do you have the protection of family and friends
the comforts of technology and the opportunity to learn?

From brainless microbes to crawling creatures of all kinds
to giant dinosaurs, to scurrying primates, to.......
The beauty that is you
The exquisite potential of thought and creativity
Of intelligence and charity

Do not waste this treasure trove,
Push yourself to accomplish good things
Smile at yourself in the mirror
And repeat that everything is going to be alright,
This is how you make the most of it all

The Earthly Castle

What is the most gracious virtue that proves your integrity?
What guides your journey, and your identity?

Nothing is more valuable than kindness-of-heart
Religions try to teach it but from this mission they depart

Lost is the goal when traditions and rituals are valued more
Then compassion and concern taking their place at the core

Insisting on dictates and interdictions
Hindering benevolence in favor of restrictions

The rules of each faith can become ends unto themselves
Forgiveness and understanding should surely be what compels

The message of true prophets has always been the same
To relinquish anger, to help one another is the perfect aim

Searching for the meaning of life so many of us have craved
Not too many have succeeded, not too many have been saved

Blind beliefs and rigidity can lead one down the road
Of delusion and self-righteousness that become the new abode

Virtue can guide us to a draw-bridge where there are waiting crowds,
But only the kind-of-heart may enter... the castle in the clouds

Shunning Negativity

We sometimes complain that there are too many regulations
That our freedoms suffer from excessive legislations

For many, without certain limitations, I have come to see
There would be a great dearth of civility

Because of so much intense personal longing
Many subconscious minds live in continuous mourning

The absence of well-being produces negative passion
Transferred to others as dislike and lack of compassion

Unhappiness appears as anger and even hatred
Imprisoned by one's ego, contradicting what should be sacred

To think the worst of others is unhealthy for the soul
It negates all virtues and even religion's goal

A fragile self always misperceives and magnifies,
Suffering and falsehoods the mind then amplifies

Hostility and blame are counterproductive
To one's own sanity, they are destructive

The greater the sadness, the more negativity is emitted
Decide to stop the self-torment and you will be delivered.

The Unmined Mind

The treasures of each mind lie in wait of being found
To emerge, to shine, to be lifted off the ground
Some glisten readily in the sun, obvious in their renown

Others in deep dark caves are locked away,
Untapped resources that never see the light of day.
They remain in musty caverns where no one hears what they say.

If no one cares to seek them out
Their unmined minds wallow in self-doubt
Sealed in the darkness of perpetual drought

A gray existence of ignorance
Suffering from others' indifference
Unable to comprehend the meaning of benevolence

Either wait to be discovered, or, burst out on your own.
Arise and materialize, face the unknown.
Whatever you imagine can become your comfort zone.

Insecurities are obstacles that you must destroy
While pursuing what you know is yours to enjoy.
Appreciating your talents will furnish needed joy.

Tarry not, for joining the cosmos will come soon enough.
Embrace all goodness and shun what is rough
Surround yourself with beauty and ignore every rebuff.

Engage in glorious creativity and of your own mind take control
As you enjoy the pure pleasure of your tender thoughtful soul.

Harmful Zeal

The need to belong is so intensely strong
To the point of sacrificing principles and even doing wrong

Ingrained since when survival depended on banding together
Existence was contingent on those of the same feather

A great pleasure indeed, to revel in that common ground
Pride in a cause and purpose finally found

When all strangers were enemies vying for land and resources,
Cohesion insured defense from perilous forces

Even today we cling to what we were taught
About exclusion and aversion to open thought

Rituals and mythology cement loyalty and exclusivity
Giving the impression that fear is needed to ensure security

The refuge of the comfort group prompts mistrust and dislike
Fulfilling a craving to belong, then making people warlike

Bitterness destroys and leads to hating others
For when anger reigns, everyone suffers

To ignore that all of life is on the same ship
Hinders the journey and poisons too, our trip

Allegiance and common sense need not be blind zeal,
Working wisely toward common goals is how we can heal

Free Will

The concept of free will might be but an invention, an illusion
With multiple levels of complexity and confusion

Are choices truly unfettered and free
Or captive in parameters impossible to flee

Pre-set preferences and aversions seem innate
Prompting every decision and action they permeate

Inescapable traits from within and without
Impede true choice as a handicap throughout

Actions are influenced more by neurons and emotions
Then by consciously weighing opposing notions

Self-mastery may help Reason to overcome passions
Harder, though, to escape generations of previous actions

Their imprint is imbedded under the skin
Luring us towards the inclinations of our kin

To know what is right yet be drawn to the rash,
Anger, the mirrored image of emotional whiplash

Virtuous is she who rows against Nature's flow
of the waters that seek their level to and fro

Needed too is a heroic strength to face the inherited obstacle,
the force that renders the notion of free will elusive and unsolvable

Stories

Unique among the many millions of earthly creatures
Storytelling is one of only mankind's features
Societies have depended on its charm since ancient times
To entertain, guide and teach, they used folklore and mimes

Human history, whether ancient or new
Is filled with accounts, though not always true
The power lies in what is remembered and conveyed
Details need not be precise if the message is well portrayed

Whether legends of heroes, or fables with moral lessons,
Mythology ruled before there were scientific professions
The mind can be a factory of fabrications,
Traditional tales were fashioned to their own specifications

Art and mythos create a subjective truth
Particular to a culture, whether refined or uncouth
Stories distract from the dreary mundane
A substitute reality to inspire the brain

To convey patterns of behavior and of feelings
Or to evade the boring quotidian dealings
Told since fire first was tamed
An intrinsic part of mankind's refrain

The ancients wove stories to cloak key information
To establish identity and explain their cultural foundation

Stories are meant to share a particular point of view
And when embraced, their mystical meaning soars blissfully anew

The Dawn

The dawn of understanding is when we first see the light.
Our ship moves in numerous continuous paths:
the daily, the yearly, the galactic and the infinite,
each realm progressively expansive.
The first, however, is the one we value most
since the dawn allows us to identify the truth:
a major source of the pain we inflict on others, and ourselves,
is the negativity that is criticism and pessimism.
The more sensitive and the more insecure,
the more one feels crushed as the life is sucked out of the soul.

When self-esteem is mangled, an ugly defense system
rages in fury, overpowering mind and body.
The victim, too, can become a perpetrator,
reenacting the harm learned from previous patterns.

There is a solution to this cycle of pain.
The answer lies in the mindful effort to filter out all disapproval:
remarks, critiques, unpleasant judgements and thoughts,
all are arrows to the ego that divest the mind of logic.

You will then reap the joys of a life without defensiveness and strife,
by sifting out every negative word, and ignoring those that you have
heard. Usher in a new existence of sweet harmony and productivity,
of calm and peace of mind.

A strong strategy, difficult indeed, but wise and rewarding once it is
achieved.

Is Anything Really Accurate

Nothing is completely accurate; nothing is as it seems.
It is all manipulation, depending on someone else's dreams.

To sound less cynical, let us then say
there are different versions that come into play.

Think back 4,000 years to Gilgamesh of Mesopotamia;
similar concerns existed then, including mythomania.

Searching for the unknowable, those questions so replete,
like him, we'll never completely find that which we seek.

So, as in ancient times, the answer has been given:
enjoy the small things of life, everything you can envision.

Be cheerful and realize the pressure is off,
you need not solve every problem that is aloft.

Surround yourself with the beauty of your choosing,
the world will remain, despite momentary bruising.

Happy is the person whose thoughts soar toward the positive.
Hope lies in striving to fashion one's own personal narrative.

Maximize the Positive

Each moment without sorrow must be celebrated, not taken for granted
Rather than the painful, continuously chanted
And the mundane, but a mist through which we float disenchanted

Let's seek to maximize the positive, optimism is the only logic
Nothing to gain only to lose by being caustic
Know yourself so as to play your hand well, that is the tonic

Be at peace with yourself by accepting your inner core
You will then have self-confidence, the key to it all
You will prosper in all things if you heed this call

Rise to the height of your individual star, uplifted
With meaning and comfort, you will then be gifted
Released from where you had previously drifted

Self-confidence lifts us from a downtrodden image
To disperse anger and defensiveness, the past sacrilege
Relationships and love no longer a distant privilege

An angry heart is love's worst obstacle
Making peace of mind and sweet connections impossible
Hostility and pessimism become diabolical

Consideration and tenderness describe love relationships
Kindness embodies the beauty of friendships
Insecurity and angry destroy such gentle partnerships

Release the rigidity and trust in your good heart
All things will then flourish and never depart

A Formula

We know what is nefarious, because it hurts,
The meaning of sin, all that perverts

Evil does damage to yourself and to others,
Can everything be sin then, everything one utters?

Are goodness and happiness too hard to attain?
Perhaps not, if this message you choose to retain.

Easy, is the river that flows, the Earth that turns,
The sun that beams, the fire that burns

Most everything else is difficult to achieve
Effort essential, and these two truths to heed:

Dwell not on the negative, we fully know its manifestations,
Focus instead on removing numbing limitations

What missing needs thwart your natural joy,
What holds back your innate longing to enjoy?

Concentrate too on a pursuit that gives life direction
That passion will provide fulfillment and connection

The rest will flow naturally as that proverbial river
With success and well-being guaranteed to deliver

Choice

Choice, not perfection, is a true and noble action
Empowered by intrinsic traits, resolution not abstraction

Following one's heart is indeed the perfect choice
To your nature's longing it gives a needed voice

Use the power to move, move away from a sorrowful place
Seek instead a more appropriate space

Embrace and expand the splendor you envision
Diminish, and wallow not, in all that brings division

Pondering at length a distorted universe,
Drags one down to focus on the perverse

Your energy is meant for a loftier aim
To influence others, to carry the flame

Surround yourself with the glory of your creations
Help others with your talents to bypass limitations

Ask for what is right, seek, and you shall find
Isn't that what He said, good advice to keep in mind

I do not question whether this be a wishful view
Or if in fact certain and true

My spirit is hopeful, and unbroken,
This because... I have chosen

Into the Garden
On the occasion of the 12th annual Belvidere Garden Tour June 2017

Waking up to a sun filled morn
Is a gift
To be valued as a precious gem

The indescribable scent of freshness,
Vapors rising up to perfume the air with nature's potion
The dazzling radiance of buds and blooms
The morning warmth upon the skin
The gentle chirping and subtle buzzing,
But most of all, Serenity.

Capture that feeling with all of your senses.
Store up its dreamy aura
Make it become part of you
Have it ready to call upon when your thoughts are racing
When disappointment strikes
When sorrowful moods choke
the body and mind.

Conjure up nature's healing power,
Step into its saving grace:
The presence of pure splendor.
Find in its flawless harmony
The strength
That sensing its existence provides.

Envelop yourself in the comfort of confidence and peace
And let it guide you
To resolution and renewal.

Chapter 2

Poetry and Science in Motion

Mankind

From tree tops and a tropical clime
to modern culture and Amazon prime

This mystery spanned many millions of years
of trial, error and countless fears

"Little Foot" was recently found,
similar to ape-like Lucy, from deep in the ground

Proportions, though, akin to modern man
just one of the many from before our time began

From primitive creatures, to thinking toolmakers
from nomadic hunters, to farmers and bread makers

10,000 years ago, another great leap of change
but advancements came at a high rate of exchange

Writing, inventions and systems of laws,
cities, armies and sorrows that wars cause

Civilizations rise and fall subject to greedy leaders' control
when people are kept ignorant, valuing only a material goal

Do you think, perhaps, the next leap might be
a new, heightened sense of sensitivity?

Education, self-discipline and awareness
Can prevent us from falling into an evolutionary abyss

As consciousness grows so too does understanding
if the brain continues learning and expanding

We all must do better, "How?", you may ask,
Promote a culture of caring, that is the task.

Turn frustration, our negative nemesis,
into kind problem-solving, make that our new Genesis.

Deep Time

What is deep time?
The very concept boggles the mind

From natural forces heavenly bodies appear
Gathering inert matter into an active sphere
With no regard for the passage of time
Indifferently creating a new paradigm

Strange names describe each eon and era
As impacts and volcanos finally form Terra
Half a billion years pass before the first spark of life
Slowly emerges from reactions and strife

A billion more, before the primordial slime
Brings forth the ancestors of future design
Oxygen from photosynthesis begins a revolution
Yet another billion years must simmer the solution

Millions of years later, sea creatures venture onto land
Adapting with roots, skin and skeletons in order to expand
Ice ages and extinctions try to quell the progress
But an explosion of life-forms now has success

Again, extinction events alter the course
Not able to stop it, but exerting a new force
65 million years ago, no longer a dinosaur threat
Mammals can diversify, the stage is now set

From cataclysms to new life, the way becomes clear
For our special species to eventually appear
7 million years ago, primate divergence occurs
Different paths our common ancestor incurs

continued

For millions of years archaic humans endure their fate
As transitional species diverge into man, from ape

A striking phenomenon is now taking place
Time seems to be accelerating its pace

From cave man to culture in mere millennia
Superstition to science is but centennial
The imbalance is dizzying, it's not easy to keep up

Slow down, plan your course, and sip your calm cup
It may all be just a rehearsal
Preparation for some cosmic reversal

Or, is it a lesson to infer how to live?
To reflect, and just make the best of what the world has to give

The Universe

Changing, Expanding, Evolving
In deep time and space imperceptibly climbing
Witnessed by the curious who find the signs
Lovers of knowledge always thirsting for finds

Awed and amazed, marveled and mystified
Stirred with emotion by the secrets crystalized
The infinitely small and the infinitely grand
Incessant interactions from star dust unplanned

Invisible powers that consume and coalesce
Furious forces that collide and compress
Or exceedingly slow ones ignoring time
Creation and devastation the directive prime

Where do we stand in all of this fury?
What is the prudent path debated by the jury?
Follow the example of Nature's resolve
And like the Universe, Move, Expand, Evolve

So, worry not, since life is such
As Kipling advises, value all, "but none too much".
In body and consciousness aim fearlessly far
For everything will pass, including our star.

The Banyan Tree

Heredity & Environment

A seed fell near a concrete wall
As time passed, it sprang up quite tall
But as its roots and branches grew
The tree and wall were no longer two
Forever entangled, they became as one
Now there's a new creation under the sun
No longer a tree like others of its kind
Changed forevermore by where it climbed

Your Own Master

So, like the unsuspecting new creation
we all grow within the confines of blueprint and location

Only certain parts of the master plan embedded in the seed
come to light, depending on what the environment has decreed

Some traits lie dormant, waiting to vivify,
most are decided by prior generations gone by

The moral is, to mold a happier reality
despite the dictates of circumstance and mentality

Fashion around you the world of your liking
or living will be dreary instead of inspiring

Not delusion, but with improvement in mind
to uplift your existence, this is triumph redefined

Invisible Forces

So many important factors that govern our lives
Are those we cannot see with naked eyes

The very air we breathe is there but invisible
Like thoughts and feelings, they are indivisible

Unseen too are atoms, gravity, the magnetic field,
Wireless signals, electricity, the ozone shield

All can be felt, but not normally seen
Without instrumentation to the extreme

Microbes, as well as the real powers that be,
Rule our lives in hidden ways we cannot see

Spirituality too, another great mystery,
so many unseen forces that guide our history

Take nothing for granted, investigate galore,
The world is full of wonders for us to explore

So much to discover, this is still the beginning,
Brave it all, and improve upon this mystery called living.

Chapter 3

Friendship and other Attachments

Freedom

Ah, the delight of the like-minded
The pure pleasure of agreement
A covenant of comfort
A bond of sweet sympathy

Not the self-effacing sort of accord
Born of tact or submission
Or the fake face of restraint
But the real kind, when you feel the love

If not, the spirit feels imprisoned
Life becomes suppressed and expressionless
The self, constantly stifled and humbled

Seek out those of a common ground
The reward will be transcendent
A life-changing liberating luxury

Lunch with Sandy

A vegan friend stopped by the other day
So I put aside my work and decided instead to play

But first I had to think really hard
To ensure that all animal products I would discard

Despite numerous items that are taboo
With a bit of thought I conjured up something new

I'm not a fan of substitute fixings
Real ingredients don our table sittings

The result abounded with color and spice
Healthy comfort without a bit of sacrifice

Copious vegetables of many hues
Garlic to dip and drinks to amuse

How we face a challenge is all in the mind
No chore is a bother for a friend who is kind

Tintinnabulation of Friends

Like chandeliers in the breeze, we sparkle and chime
Protected by a pergola of intertwining vine

Just overhead, lifted above worldly harm
We sway together in fragrant summerlike charm

Individual in design yet sharing spirit and passions
We revel in the harmony our "ring of bells" fashions

A joyful reverberating symphony
A rescue from the mundane through sympathy

Inspiration away from the clang of the uncouth
Assuring comfort and perpetual youth

A refuge from the enmity of ignorance and the venom of vexation.
Where is this safe place, this calming habitation?

None other than the realm of our relationship,
The glittering crystal that is our Friendship

Goddess Friends

Come gather now around the fire
Goddesses all, tis time to conspire

Beauty and Wisdom your aura dispenses
Like sweet perfume reaching our senses

Never doubt the power of your influence
No need to anger at others' insolence

They are merely living within their bounds
So different from what in you resounds

May our pantheon lift us to a higher plane
From the depths of the profane to our grand domain

Peace of Mind

We both look at something, but perceive it in a different way
In fact, all that we are, will come into play

Our emotional disposition, background and experiences
Influence and shape our reality and differences

What exists for one, I'm sure you realize,
Takes quite a different shape when seen through another's eyes

When emotions flare and feelings rage
A self-inflicted war takes center stage

Only self-confident calm, and shared respect
Will restore peace of mind and allow us to reconnect

Scheherazade

I shudder to think that romantic ties
often end with the pain of love's demise.

Moments of elation, endless expectation,
then doubt and disappointment tumbling to frustration.

Ironically, each individual's sensitive self
lacks the skill to secure its own emotional health

As littered remains of rose petal fantasies
flutter to the ground as wilted profanities.

Ah, Scheherazade knew how to escape that fate.
Versed in the fine arts, she created a constant curious state.

Her stories entranced the king, his interest was sparked,
soon he could no longer bear to be apart

With charm and intelligence, she ended his cruel reign.
He became a wiser man, loving and humane.

This transformation came on the wings of a dove,
for goodness must flourish for the heart to know love.

The Story of Tea Time with 8-year-old Luca 2017

So there in the garden we sat, Luca and I, in the most idyllic Tea Time setting:
warm air perfumed with honeysuckle and jasmine, Debussy playing in the background, Nature's pink and yellow jewels sparkling in the morning sun, as we discussed fables of Aesop and La Fontaine and other poetic parables.

All at once, smack, bam, a jolt of reality:
so incongruous was Luca's comment that all we could do was laugh, and laugh at great length, we did.

In utter contrast to the sublimity of the moment, Luca pointed out that the picture on the apricot jelly jar looked like, as he described it, "someone's butt". "Humm", said I, "that hit me with a bit of unexpected earthiness". Luca's response made it all worthwhile. "Well," he said, "I just got struck by living with a smile forever".

Luca's Visit During
The Spring of the Pandemic 2020

I feel a tinge of guilt these days to be of such cheery mien
While others all around me fret a bleak uneasy scene.

How strange that this halt in many usual events
Has allowed for creative deeds that make delightful sense.

Let's reminisce in our special way,
And list some activities we do each day:

To awake as without a care in the world,
Bursting as a brilliant flag unfurled;

To await the pure pleasures of discovery and art;
To notice the varied daffodils that uplift the heart

Then to draw them and recite their poetry
 "Wandering lonely as a cloud", so lovingly;

To hike and bike and dance in carefree peace
Along the path and river's edge that seem to never cease

Then to return home to sauce and spice our culinary delights
As Tchaikovsky in the background lifts us up to greater heights;

To live the gentle genteel life
Without a hint of woe or strife.

All this springs from our bond of sweet trust,
Come, my boy, let's make that pie with extra crust.

To Phil

Too often we have the habit
Of not appreciating something when we have it

Like you, Phil, for instance
For you are truly a man of substance

Passionate and honest in your search for the truth
Politics, and all evils, burdens since your youth

Protective and generous, forever willing to assist
On goodness of heart, you would always insist

Longingly, a better world you implore
For the dear grandchildren you so adore

A bond with Susan so deep and strong
"Because You Loved Me", your sweet song

You were blessed to love each other,
Facing the world as a comforting buffer

A heart so kind
A hero's mind

Searching for the ideal
With lofty values, yet humble you feel

Disappointed by lies
A gentleman in disguise

We love you Phil
And we always will

The Farm
A True Story

We bought a Farm
That has no Barn

We bought some land
Without a farm-hand

The well runs deep
But drawing the water will be a feat

There are no crops
On the empty plots

The road up the mountain is unpaved
Yet to gain access, it must be braved

There is, however, a huge saving grace:
Hamou has finally found his longed-for place

His mind's eye can already see
The lemon trees that someday will be

The expansive view of the Mediterranean Sea
Is truly an inspiration, says he

It is the realization of a dream
The culmination of his life's theme

The fantasy is no longer remote
Soon he will sail his beloved boat

Deep Discussion over Morning Coffee

What thinkest thou, my sweet, he asked,
Delighted, she gushed forth quite unabashed,

"The many ways we now can see
What once was cloaked in obscurity

The collective effort to reveal, unseal, discover and invent
To clarify, demystify and unearth what is meant

The desire to explain phenomena as in ancient times
But only imagined elucidations were written in their lines

Slowly, knowledge is unmasking what used to be unseen
The invisible, before science, was behind a magic screen

The physical and philosophical no longer superstition
Unveiling the mysteries of the Universe is now the mission

This understanding can surely benefit all of us
if only it is not ignored by those we're supposed to trust."

How lucky, she thought, that he listened to her ramblings so lovingly
And how she appreciated his devotion so very abundantly.

Confidenza

A pleasure to appreciate, summed up in one word,
"Confidenza", the greatest gift to be conferred

The feeling of elation when a sweet bond is struck
Connection and shared perception, a joy left seemingly to luck

The comfort of being oneself without judgment or mistrust
For Happiness and well-being, undoubtedly a must

Pour praise upon those kindred spirits as nurturing a cherished orchid
They energize the soul and ease away all that is sordid

For some, your efforts are wasted droplets absorbed into the sand
Be not offended by those fellows, for they do not understand

They were led astray by misfortunes endured before
And thus, barely to blame, rather to ignore

Not to make excuses or bemoan a sorry state
But to amend through wisdom, a predetermined fate

Aversion from some, recognition from others
Save your emotion for the gentle words that someone utters

"Confidenza" is a joy akin to Greek agape'
Soothing approval that validates you on your way

Plenteous or plain, possessions or paucity,
"Confizenda" affords the soul equal generosity

Ode a` ma belle-mère

Mars 2020

Et belle elle est, en effet
Pour sa personne et pour tout ce qu'elle fait

Pure d'esprit, pieuse et forte
Le paradis surement lui ouvrira ses portes

Elle mérite l'estime de nous tous
Car malgré les moments durs, elle reste douce

Mère d'une tribu, nous lui devons notre admiration
Pour ses sacrifices, pour sa dévotion

Toujours serviable dans sa captivité
Dès un jeune âge elle en a fait un palais

Prête à se sacrifier par son courage
Respectée par ses enfants et par son entourage

Elle a toujours pensé aux autres au dépens d'elle-même
Mon seul désir c'est qu'elle m'aime

Honnête, franche et valeureuse
Travailleuse et aussi toujours généreuse

Comme récompense nous lui offrons des louanges
Car elle couve ceux qu'elle chérie comme un ange

Le pilier et le guide de toute la famille
Son âme entière elle y a mis

Elle mérite que nous l'apprécions
Et avec reconnaissance, de tout cœur, nous l'aimons

Chapter 4

A Few Dark Moments

Delight and Heartache Inflicted by Love

The diamond - symbol of commitment and love
Signifying a happily-ever-after union from above

What fantasy and delusion
What fertile ground for disappointment and confusion

The truth be told, it marks but the start
Of an arduous process, a battle of the heart

A journey of tender learning, yet believing in the ideal
Disappointment and elation, both feelings are real

That one faux pas makes you want to shout out
that one drop of espresso darkens your doubt

Emotional nausea can grip the heart and throat
From obliviously committed slights or an inane joke

Heed this hovering spirit, and know that the "ideal"
Must be taught and learned to seal the deal

Use every obstacle as an opportunity for growth
Require behavior that reassures you of his oath

When your knight falls from his steed, roll your eyes and your sleeves
Again and again until your vision he perceives

Detach your ego from any pain
A higher level of love you will ultimately gain

Disappointed

This I have lived, or dreamed it in a nightmare
Heavy is the burden for those who ponder and care

If it flows onto you, my patient paper friend
Will it impart sweet peace by leaving in the end?

The dangerous egos of unhappy souls
Gather all around as frightening foes

Insecurities evinced by bitter deeds
Vengeful jealousy their heart often heeds

To those here below their countenance is a curse
Instead of according importance, confine them to a mere verse

Their troubles may be many, their minds in torment
Pity their affliction for they'll never be content

Their potential wondrous, if they could trust in their own worth
Perhaps then, would emerge kindness and mirth

For now, only suspicion and self-interest reign
Like pelting icy hail adding sadly to my pain

L'Esprit

Make a good friend of me or I will torment your every moment, your
restless sleep too.
I race in all directions, but I am the constant companion that never
says "adieu".
I will haunt your deepest thoughts and make you doubt yourself with
fear,
no peace will be yours until I am controlled, since I will always be
near.

Can you make me wise, disciplined and kind?
The tools of intellect and virtue can you help me find?
It may be a life-long endeavor, but well worth the time,
for what is more important than purpose and peace of mind?

If not, every perception will rely solely on petty emotion,
good and evil grounded only in personal devotion,
constantly shadowed by jealousy and distain,
discerning between truth and manipulation an impossible gain.

Meditate, medicate, intoxicate all you want,
if left feral, I will always be there waiting to taunt
when distractions are fleeting and sleep is disturbed
by an anxious energy that is never curbed.

The good-hearted, only if secure and confident,
can enjoy the supernal benefits and be content.
They avoid all extremes whether virtue or vice.
They embrace calm and logical thinking at any price.

You have, perhaps, guessed who I must be,
I'm your inescapable mind, "ton esprit".

Self-destruction, or mastery and glory?
Choose well, to ensure a happy ending to your story.

Emotional Pain

This is what people in pain do
They can't help rehashing, they eschew what is new

Over and over, they mull over the same load
From fear and self-doubt their minds implode

They blame themselves even when no one else will
To the point of destruction, they become increasingly ill

Fight that consuming passion by repeating a new mantra
A bolstering army of a different genre

Use the same repetitious tactic but now in reverse
Repeating your praises will then lift the curse

The world will continue on with your worry or without
Praise yourself instead, whenever in doubt

Unfetter your grip in order to find peace
It's someone else's turn, that will secure your release

When agonizing thoughts again flood the brain
Block them by repeating a positive personal refrain

Problems will always exist, that, our consciousness ensures
But uncontrollable worry will prevent all cures

It's a battle against oneself; no one else is there inside
Making it all the worse, for there is nowhere to hide

Continued

The sorrow and pain, they come from within
Recall instead the good you've done, not the chagrin

Despite heroic efforts, the cards will fall where they may
It will all work out, even if not quite your way

When you take a step back, others will pick up the slack
You are not at fault for what others lack

Obsessive rehashing provides no solution
Other than adding to one's dreadful confusion

Reject self-destruction at any cost
Value yourself first or all will be lost

Forgive yourself completely; you are not to blame
Only then will you loosen the strangling chain

Life Not Enjoyed

Similar to the preparation, presentation and partaking
Of a flavorsome culinary endeavor,
Forgotten, completely and immediately once the last morsel is
consumed

Unmemorable because
Emotional receptors are clogged
With the toxins of self-centered thoughtlessness

Mimicking a robotic entity, guarded,
Going through the motions without showing emotion
Protecting an inner core of selfish sensitivity

Content in its own way, yet
Contrary to mindfulness,
Taking every gift for granted

Ignoring so much that could be enjoyed
Oblivious to the closeness lost
Missing the opportunities served on a glistening tray

All is lost, until he sees
The joys of consciousness uplifted,
The sublime union waiting to be gifted

Borderline

A subtle annoyance
A slow simmer kept under a lid
The steam bubbling, impossible to ignore

Enough to mar the moment
Enough to prickle the skin
Enough to anger the soul and make it cringe

Impatience and defensiveness personified
A compost pile of unhappiness
Spews its fertilizer on every situation

Toxic fumes alter the brain cells
To interpret with evil perspective

To tolerate would be to reward
To accept would mean to validate
To overlook would only encourage more

Distracting me from the positive
Preventing forward movement
Tarnishing my peace
Saddening my countenance
wasting my time

Awaken, give more, you can.
Will it and make it so.
All good things will come to you in return.

Chapter 5

Freedom in the Sun

Cap Cana 2017

The sails of the Catamaran filled with nature's sweet breath
and propelled us along a blissful cyan trail

Peacock colored tips on sunburnt limbs splashed up ever-changing
white water formations along our aqua path

Even though a hurricane may loom in the distance, for this moment
in time, all is calm and peaceful

This splendor, imbibed, absorbed and stored, will help us weather
the storms of life that may lie ahead

One Miami Moment

Ten pink flower petals
ripple slowly
below the surface of turquoise waters

moving peacefully
in the warm breezy glow of pure light

liquid tranquility
engulfs the body
in its comforting caress

Sail Quest

The sails of the "Cosmic Arrow" billow
As her bow pierces the realm below

Tiny points of light sparkle all around
Appearing and disappearing at the whim of the wind

The horizon in the distance soon becomes one with the heavens

Exulted by Nature's incomprehensible mysteries
Floating, flying, entering into a vast expanse as if to the stars above

Guided by celestial winds, the Unknown beckons
To the adventurous vulnerable voyager

Early Morning on the Terrace of Bahia Principe, DR

Black bird on a white wicker chair
Calling and clamoring in the warm morning air

The bird ever-so-black, the chair a blinding white
Yet, that's Nature's way, so it must be right

Contrast inspires life and makes feelings abound
Goodness in all things can surely be found

The Earth moves, time divides into day and night
It is natural to live with darkness and light

When hearts are open to Beauty, it truly will exist
Create it, embrace it and always persist

Cuidado Khalida

Cuidado when bronzing under the broiling sun.
Like all luring dangers, it first appears as fun.

Be careful lest it drain you of your life-force,
spinning your brain completely off course,

hardly able to walk, skin burning yet cold,
your head a red giant ready to explode.

Every excess begins with a high,
then often leaves one wanting to cry.

Only harsh experience can this lesson teach,
may your compensation be, a perfect turquoise beach!

Secrets Beach, DR 2018

Grateful is she who can pen a happy verse
The heart clear and light, not one thought perverse

The ills of the world may be many
Right now, I cannot perceive any

At this moment in time, beauty conquers all
A breeze of perfect warmth and a beach to enthrall

Never again to take such good fortune for granted
To submerge and soak up a place so enchanted

The sun and scene dazzle as bodies bronze
Crystal blue surrounds us beneath soaring palms

The array of bare skin amazes with its many hues
Overflowing beachwear boundaries, or sporting tattoos

White to black, myriad shades of brown in-between
All here to escape and blur their work routine

No longer separated by earthly limits
Here to enjoy these precious Caribbean minutes